This Notebook Belongs To:

_____

NAME

How to use this journal

In order to get the best out of this journal, you should commit to working through the thirty days by reading and doing the activities every day for thirty days. There are blank note pages at the end of each day which you can use to expand on your thoughts and ideas. There is a list of affirmations at the end of the journal for daily use. As a start, choose a few which speaks to what you are currently experiencing or what you would like to change. Add or change as you so wish. Use the blank pages at the back for your own journaling experience. Enjoy!

Introduction

I believe that we all want to be happy, to change our circumstances for the better and to make a difference in people's lives. And we can, but what usually keep us back are the thoughts we think, the negative self-belief and the self-limiting choices we make.

How do we make a change in the direction of accomplishing our dreams and desires? Do we even have dreams?

The purpose of this journal-book is to help you to reflect on yourself, who you want to become and guides you through the key areas of focus to help you shape who you are becoming, to blossom into the young lady and woman you can admire, to live a vibrant, authentic, loving, influential and enjoyable teenage life.

I ask that you commit to the 30 days of self-development by reading and completing the activities. Use the blank pages provided to write down your own thoughts. Practice the affirmations at the back of the journal. You should also try discussing what you've learned with family and friends.

I wish you well, I wish you a beautiful life, I wish you continuous improvement.

God bless.

Daneile

Who am I?

First things first, do you know you are created in the image of God? Yes, God; the creator of heaven and earth. How cool is that?! Take a moment and let that sink in. Meditate on it. Close your eyes and say it over and over and over and over again (see the activity below).

ACTIVITY

Repeat this affirmation 20 times, in the state of calmness and mindfulness.
"I am created in the image of God."
Now open your eyes. How do you feel?

....

....

What do you think is the "image" of God? And, how can this empower you?

....

....

QUOTE:

> "I will praise you for I am fearfully and wonderfully made;
> marvelous are your works and that my soul knows very well."
> —Psalms 139:14.

100% Responsibility

Taking 100% responsibility for your life means you take ownership of your decisions and accept the consequences of your actions. It also means that you are not a victim; but rather you are the creator of your future.

This doesn't mean if someone hurts you, it's your fault! You are not responsible for anyone's behavior. However, you are responsible for your reaction. If someone does hurt you, speak out for yourself. Report it if you have to but most importantly, do the inner work of forgiving and moving forward. Focusing on the other person can only make you angrier, so resolving, forgiving, and moving forward become the ideal position.

Taking 100% responsibility for your life gives you power! Because, if you have the power to make the decisions you made, then you also have the power to make different choices and these new choices will set you on the path to creating the results you want. Isn't that wonderful?

ACTIVITY

1. In what areas do I need to take 100% responsibility for my life?

....

....

2. How will this change the way I perceive life?

....

....

QUOTE:

"To achieve major success in life, you must accept 100% responsibility for your life. Nothing less will do"
—Jack Canfield.

NOTES

A girl with Goals

One of the best things you can do for yourself is to set goals. Goals give you immense focus and help in creating an amazing life. *Note*: For this to be effective, your goals must be written down and reviewed regularly. Studies show that goals with timelines attached are far more likely to be realized. Here's an example to guide you in setting your goals.

Compare Sharon and Chelsea's goal:

Sharon: I would like to participate at my school's championships.

Chelsea: I will compete in the 100m race at my school's championship in November 2021.

Did you notice the difference? Sharon wants to participate but has not decided on a specific race or time. Unlike Sharon, Chelsea has settled on one particular event and has gathered all the relevant details about the race.

ACTIVITY

Write down three specific goals that you want and will commit to achieving. Remember to follow the guidance above.

....

....

....

....

QUOTE:

"Write your list of goals down in detail and read your list every day"
—Jack Canfield.

NOTES

I Believe

All things are possible to them that believe. In order to achieve anything, you first must believe that it is possible. When you really believe something can be done your mind find ways to get it done. Belief fuels your soul to never lose hope no matter what the present circumstances suggest. When you make it your habit to always believe in yourself and the fact that God is rooting for you, you eventually create your realities. There is a saying that goes like this; "if you can believe it, you can achieve it". Well, the opposite is also true. If you cannot believe it, you cannot achieve it.

Useful tips to believing in yourself and your dreams:

- Treat yourself as someone you deeply love
- Visualize your life as if your dreams are already a reality and act as though they are
- Set goals and take consistent action to achieve them
- Remain faithful when times get tough. Don't give up!

ACTIVITY

On a scale of one to ten, how much would you rate yourself as believing in yourself and your future?

....

....

How do you see yourself in the future? Are you happy, sad, working for the government, dancing in front of thousands of people, singing at weddings?

....

....

QUOTE:

"You become what you believe" —Oprah Winfrey

"Nothing is impossible. The word itself says "I'm possible"."
—Audrey Hepburn

My thoughts

Having positive thoughts is important because they change your world! Thoughts become your reality. Whatever you focus on, expands.

Keep negative thoughts out by surrounding yourself with positivity.

And remember, it wouldn't happen overnight! Keep at it!

ACTIVITY

1. Pay attention to your thoughts. Throughout today, monitor what you're thinking about. If you entertain positive thoughts, Keep it that way! If not, make a conscious effort to replace those negative thoughts with some positivity.

Example:

Initial thought: I have to complete my science project, but I have no one to help me. I will fail.

Change to: I have to complete my science project. I may have no help, but I'm great at researching new topics so I know I'm going to get this done with an A grade!

2. In which areas am I most negative - my classes, my body, or my family?

....

....

3. What positive things can I think about to turn away from negative thinking and embrace positive thinking?

....

....

QUOTE:

"Thoughts become things....Choose the good ones!"
—Mike Dooley.

NOTES

Gratitude

Practicing gratitude everyday must be priority. Gratitude is being grateful for everything in your life. Feeling grateful for what you have instead of obsessing with what you don't have opens up doors for more blessings.

Gratitude also improves your mood; it helps you gain perspective in difficult decisions.

ACTIVITY:

What gracious habit can I start now? For example, praying before meals and before sleep.

....

....

What are some things in my life that I can be grateful for that I may not have paid any attention to? For example, do you have electricity in your home or, do you have running water? Many people around the world live without these necessities that we often take for granted.

....

....

QUOTE:

"Gratitude opens the door to the power, the wisdom, the creativity of the universe" —Deepak Chopra.

NOTES

Darling, you're different

This is not just a saying, it's actually very true. No one is exactly like you. You were created special. It's a waste of time to wish you were someone else. You cannot be them and they certainly cannot be you. It's time to celebrate your uniqueness. That's right! There's no need to brag when someone gives you a compliment. Smile and say thank you. If you're a talented baker, practice your skill, keep learning more, share your goodies with friends and family.

And remember you're not only your outward beauty, your talents, characteristics and faith all make up who you are.

You're a limited edition!

ACTIVITY

In what situations do I find myself comparing to others?

....

....

How can I avoid this, and focus on being myself instead?

....

....

The one best unique thing about me is?

....

....

QUOTE:

"You have to be unique & different to shine in your own way."
—Lady Gaga

"Why fit in when you were born to stand out?" —Dr. Seuss

NOTES

My beautiful Body

You take your body with you everywhere you go! Yes, your body is your ally, always there for you. Isn't that enough a reason to love and care for it?

Many times we say things like: I wish my legs were thinner, I don't like my eyes, or even more startling ones like I hate my nose! Just think about it: your nose allows you to appreciate and not appreciate all the smells around you, your eyes will enable you to see and experience the world through vivid color, while your legs take you places. See what I mean? So, it's essential to love and appreciate every inch of you, appreciate all your beautiful parts.

It's also vital to take care of your body through eating healthy foods and regular exercise.

ACTIVITY

Use this affirmation daily: I am beautiful in every single way.

List 6 aspects you love about your body.

I love ....

I love ....

I love ....

I love ....

I love ....

I love ....

QUOTE:

"Adore your body, for it houses the dreams and the desires of your wonderful mind." —Unknown

My self-esteem

Self-esteem refers to the way you feel about yourself, what you think is your worth. Self-esteem translates to self-worth. It affects your happiness, your grades, the way you stand up for yourself and everything else you do.

Low self-esteem will have you doubting your abilities, your beauty, and your worth. Low self-esteem demands other people's approval of your life. It screams that your opinion of yourself is not good enough.

When you have low self-esteem, you think negatively, and do so regularly. But don't believe the lies in your head; you were born with purpose and with inbuilt talents which constitute what it takes to accomplish amazing things.

Some tips for improving your self-esteem:

- Celebrate your strengths and successes
- speak positively about yourself
- Set goals and work towards them
- Stay away from negative people
- Give and help others in need
- Be kind to yourself

ACTIVITY

My positive qualities are: ....

....

What do friends and family like most about me? ....

....

What are some characteristics I like in others that I also have? ....

....

We all have things to work on. What do I need to work on? ....

....

QUOTE:

"Your self-worth is determined by you. You don't have to depend on someone telling you who you are." —Beyonce

Mirror Work

Do you know that many people don't look into the mirror? This is because they don't like what they see. Practice looking into the mirror and deep into your eyes. Say, "I love you. I really really love you!" Do this every morning and every night.

If you have a pocket mirror you should carry it around in your bag. Use it whenever you can.

After a while of saying nice words to yourself consistently, you will believe them deep down. And no one will be able to shake this foundation of self-love from you.

ACTIVITY

Take a moment now to carry out this exercise. It may feel awkward at first, but once you do it for a few minutes and repeat, it will feel just fine. Say your name............ followed by "I love you. I love you so much." These are the right signals to send to your subconscious mind.

Write down how you feel afterward.

....

....

QUOTE:

"Talk to yourself like you would to someone you love."
—Brene Brown.

NOTES

Reflecting

There is considerable value to be found in reflecting about our friends, family, school and choices. Think about what you have done so far. What could have been done better, in what areas have you really excelled? This type of reflection provides you with feedback, which helps you to be appreciative of what you have and what you've been through. Also, it provides a foundation on which to build future goals.

It's good if you can plan to regularly practice reflection. You can say: every Sunday morning I will spend some time reflecting or, every first Sunday of each month.

ACTIVITY

Am I still doing what I believe in?

....

....

How am I doing in my studies or career?

....

....

How do I feel about the friends in my life? Are they making me better?

....

....

What do I really like doing?

....

....

QUOTE:

"Without reflection, we go blindly on our way, creating more unintended consequences, and failing to achieve anything useful."
—Margaret J. Wheatley.

Handling Rejection

Everybody likes to feel accepted by the people they like, people who they perceive as important, the popular kids and such. When this doesn't happen, we can feel ignored or rejected.

Understand today that it is not practical to always have everyone's approval. And it is not important to have their approval! What matters is what you think of yourself, do you approve of you!

ACTIVITY

Write a list of all your great, positive and strong characteristics. When you remind yourself about all the positive things in your life, you will be able to overcome rejection better.

a. ....

b. ....

c. ....

d. ....

e. ....

f. ....

QUOTE:

"There are no real successes without rejection.
The more rejection you get, the better you are, the more you've learned, the closer you are to your outcome...
If you can handle rejection, you'll learn to get everything you want"
—Tony Robbins.

NOTES

the leader in me

You were born to lead! Although you may not have a title or be the leader of your youth club or sports team, you possess leadership qualities. Being a leader means you have a majority of the following attributes:

- A knack for excellence and effectiveness.
- Motivational and inspirational demeanor.
- Respect for self and for others.
- Positive and forward-thinking.
- You're not afraid to express your opinion.
- A team player.
- Discipline.

You may be wondering why you should be thinking of leadership at such a young age. But practicing and developing leadership qualities will help you become more confident, perform better in school, take on new challenges and make positive contributions to your family and community as a whole. In a nutshell, you will get to live a more fulfilling and enjoyable life.

ACTIVITY

Which quality can I improve today?

....

....

In what ways will this help me?

....

....

QUOTE:

"The youth of today are leaders of tomorrow." —Nelson Mandela.

fear versus faith

Fear is really false facts appearing real. Faith is believing in your heart that something good is going to happen.

Fear has a way of holding you back from accomplishing your dreams and goals, keeping you from trying new things. In contrast, faith allows you to push towards your dreams. It gives you the confidence to believe that you have what it takes and enables you to believe that in the end, you will achieve what you set out to accomplish.

You can build your faith by two key ways:

- Allow yourself to try something new, even if the path and outcomes are uncertain. Once you've done it, you will feel more confident.
- Pray and read the scriptures. Faith-filled words will help you feel more positive about yourself and your circumstances.

ACTIVITY

Describe a time when you felt fearful but did what you had to do anyway.

....

....

How did you feel after?

....

....

What did you learn from this?

....

....

QUOTE:

"I say I am stronger than fear." —Malala Yousafzai

"Faith can move mountains" —The Bible: Matthew 17:20

Any ideas of what Hope is? Hope is believing that there is light despite of all the darkness we see around us.

If you're experiencing difficulties (everyone does), hope is what keeps you going, believing that the situation is not permanent and that eventually, something is going to change. You may not know what will change but you know it will come to change when the time is right. Commit to remain hopeful.

Practicing deep breathing, visualization, gratitude Journaling, Prayer and creative arts can all help in maintaining hopefulness.

ACTIVITY

What does it feel like to be hopeful?

....

....

Which situations require me to be hopeful right now?

....

....

QUOTE:

"Don't be afraid. Be focused. Be determined.
Be Hopeful. Be empowered." —Michelle Obama.

NOTES

Bloom like a rose

Have you noticed how the flowers bloom in the garden? When you get a chance, take a look outside and admire the flowers. They always seem so radiant and beautiful. Guess what! They are doing what they are supposed to do! And you can do the same too! Bloom wherever you're at.

If you're in high school, university, or any other higher learning institution, focus on excelling there. Don't think that you will do better once you get to the next level of studies. Do your best now! In whatever stage of life you're at, bloom! Always try your best, maintain a smile on your face and be kind to others.

ACTIVITY

How can I add more joy to what I'm doing?

....

....

Affirmation: God has given me the power to enjoy what I'm working on. I'll bloom right here, right now.

QUOTE:

"Wherever you are, know that God has put you there for a reason" —Joel Osteen

NOTES

Dream, always

Dreams are free! And guess what! You get to have as many as you want. As big and outrageous as you wish.

Having dreams are the first step to creating a beautiful life for yourself. It is important to note that it takes effort on your part to make your dreams a reality. Once you have your dreams in place, set goals that are in line with bringing them to reality.

A good idea is to group your dreams into categories, for example education, career, hobbies, financial and health. If you have dreams and goals in all areas of your life you will increase your chances of happiness.

ACTIVITY

What have you been dreaming of lately? Write down your major dreams. Remember to be clear and precise.

....

....

Continue on a separate page if you need to, writing down as many as possible. Feel free to change them as you grow and encounter new experiences.

QUOTE:

"The future belongs to those who believe in the beauty of their dreams" —Eleanor Roosevelt

"If you can dream it, you can do it." —Walt Disney

Giving Back

Giving back makes the world a better place. Giving does not have to be in the form of money; it can be volunteering at church, a community group or a school project.

Volunteering provides a means of learning new skills such as; working with a team, making new friends and making a difference in the lives of people. Also, the fact that you are helping someone else is highly empowering and it helps to make you happier.

It's important to start wherever you're at right now. If you practice giving when you don't have much, you're more likely to give when you do have a lot.

Some benefits of giving:

- Giving to others makes us feel happy
- Giving connects us with other people
- Giving often brings feelings of gratitude

ACTIVITY

Do you practice giving? If yes, how do you do it?

....

....

Do you volunteer? If yes, how?

....

....

Why is volunteering important to your community?

....

....

QUOTE:

"No one has ever become poor by giving" —Anne Frank

"Giving back is always in style" —Unknown

NOTES

Confidence

Confidence is your superpower!

Most of us do not take time to analyse our talents and strengths. We go around admiring everyone else, which can sometimes lead to a lack of confidence in our own abilities. We tend to place more focus on what we think we are lacking.

Confidence is developed in two main ways:

Firstly, by doing difficult things. Try things that seem too difficult for you. If you're fearful, do it anyways.

Secondly, confidence is developed by keeping the promises we make to ourselves.

Please note, that anyone can develop confidence! You just have to work at it every single day.

ACTIVITY

Make a list of the things you like about yourself, for example: I love my smile; I can cook very well.

....

....

Decide on one thing you can do to create more confidence in yourself. For example, I will read my school books for one hour every evening.

....

....

I feel more confident when   ....

I will feel more confident if I   ....

QUOTE:

"When you have confidence you can have a lot of fun. And when you have fun, you can do amazing things" —Joe Namath.

Trustworthiness

People admire persons who are trustworthy. It means they are honest, reliable and responsible. People will like you and want to do things with you if they view you as trustworthy.

Trustworthiness is a characteristic trait that will help you long past your teen years. It will help you on your first job, on sport teams, on volunteering assignments and such endeavors.

Some ways to become trustworthy:

• Keep secrets, especially when asked to by the person telling you
• Be kind and compassionate
• Always Keep your word
• Always be honest

ACTIVITY

Are you honest in your words and actions?

....

....

Do you keep your promises?

....

....

Do you stand up for what you believe in and always do what's right, no matter the price?

....

....

QUOTE:

"No legacy is as rich as honesty" —William Shakespeare

NOTES

Friendships

Friendships are essential for your development. Real friends help you get through a crisis or rough time. They provide a listening ear and shoulder to cry on when needed. Above all these, you get a sense of acceptance and belonging, just by having friends.

If you have good friends, that's great! But if not, you can try being a friend to someone. There's a saying that goes like this, "show me your company and I'll tell you who you are." So, choose your friends wisely. Friends that are honest, respectful and working towards their goals will be a positive influence in your life.

ACTIVITY

Take a moment to reflect on your friendships.

Which friends are closest to you, and what do you like most about them?

....

....

How do you and your friends make each other better?

....

....

Do you proactively select your friends?

....

....

QUOTE:

> "True friends are like diamonds- bright, beautiful, valuable, and always in style." —Nicole Richie

NOTES

Money Habits

Money may not be a popular topic among young people, but for sure, it needs to be. Having money of your own gives a sense of freedom and confidence. Money gives you options! It would be a great advantage if you learn how to save and manage your money from now.

You must aim to save a portion of all the funds that come into your hands. If you have a part-time job or you receive an allowance, make sure you don't spend it all. If possible, discuss opening a bank account with your parents. This way you can do regular savings with little access to spending it out.

In order to be financially independent, you must practice saving and other good financial habits.

ACTIVITY

Do I currently have any money? How much? ....
....

What are my sources (job, parents..) of income? ....
....

How can I start saving or saving more? ....
....

What are my financial goals? For example, I am saving in order to attend a summer camp. ....
....

How can I increase my knowledge about managing money? ....
....

QUOTE:

> "Do not save what is left after spending;
> spend what is left after saving." —Warren Buffet

NOTES

Integrity

It's a good time to develop integrity. This is a vital quality that will move you towards accomplishing all that is required. Integrity basically means that you keep your word even if no one is watching.

People like being around people of integrity. It will help you on a job and also, in maintaining good friendships.

Make it a habit to do whatever you say you'll do. Keep your promises made to people. And if for some reason you can't, always inform them of the situation.

ACTIVITY

Do you feel like you are a person of integrity?

....

....

How can you become even better?

....

....

QUOTE:

"Honor your commitments with Integrity."
—Les Brown

Express your feelings

Expressing your feelings is important to your mental health. It's better to talk to someone about a situation than to let it fester until you explode. If a friend offends you, you should speak to them about it. If nothing changes, at least you expressed it and can make decisions without feeling bad about them.

When you start speaking up for yourself, you will notice you feel better about yourself. You'll feel more confident. Like you're taking control of your life.

ACTIVITY

How do I feel about my life in general?

....

....

How do I feel about the way people treat me?

....

....

Do you sometimes feel like you should speak up more or speak up sooner?

....

....

QUOTE:

"Don't keep your feelings sheltered, express them.
Don't ever let life shut you up." —Dr Steve Maraboli.

NOTES

Developing the Right Habits

What do you think is a habit? It's the things we do daily without much thought. It feels like we're doing them automatically. For example, when you wake up, what's the first thing you do? Perhaps you go to the bathroom to brush your teeth or maybe you have your shower and then brush your teeth. You do things in this order every day or most days. These are habits.

Some habits are neutral but some habits are also good and some are bad. A good habit could be that you exercise every morning before going off to school. A bad habit could be walking into your classroom without saying good morning to the kids in the room or waiting until the very last evening to do an assignment before it is due.

ACTIVITY

Which of your habits do you like most?

....

....

Which habits would you like to get rid of and why?

....

....

What new habits would you like to form and how will they improve your life?

....

....

QUOTE:

"Good habits formed at youth make all the difference."
—Aristotle.

Self-Discipline

Self-discipline is your ability to do and act like you plan to **whether you feel like it or not**. Discipline can sound like a bad word! But it's actually a very good word, a freedom word. When you develop self-discipline in any area of your life, you create time to work on other things.

Discipline is also a confidence builder because it gets you to do difficult things. To accomplish your goals, you'll need self-discipline. It is like a muscle, if you practice every day you'll find that you're becoming better.

ACTIVITY

Do you consider yourself disciplined at the moment? Why?

....

....

What will I do, starting today, to develop self-discipline?

(Start small. For example, make up your bed as soon as you wake up every single day.)

....

....

QUOTE:

"At the center of bringing any dream into fruition is self-discipline." —Will Smith.

NOTES

Courage

Courage is an internal quality that has nothing to do with how you look! Courageous is being able to ask questions in class while everyone else is looking at you with the weird eye. Courageous is trying out for the school's team while risking the awful "No!" Courageous is saying no to friends even though you may be rejected. Courageous is speaking up to bullies when you see them being unkind to the quiet kid in school.

Being courageous is a wonderful quality to aim for. If you feel like you're not courageous, you can practice by trying new things as often as you can and by speaking up for yourself.

ACTIVITY

Describe a time when you had the courage to do the right thing even though you were fearful.

....

....

In what areas would I like to be more courageous? And how can I practice being courageous?

....

....

QUOTE:

"Success is not final; failure is not fatal.
It is the courage to continue
that counts." —Unknown.

 Resilient

Resilience is the ability to bounce back from adversity. When you are resilient, you do not easily crack under pressure.

Life will throw many opportunities at you that require resilience! Whether failure at school, loss of someone you love or sickness. Be determined to be resilient whenever you face obstacles.

There is just something captivating about a girl who is an overcomer! She accomplishes her goals despite being knocked down. She always finds ways to get back up whenever her goals are challenged.

ACTIVITY

When have you experienced a setback, failure or disappointment and how did the experience make you feel?

....

....

How did you overcome it?

....

....

How do you feel knowing that you are able to get over that?

....

....

QUOTE:

"Never, never, never, never give up" —Winston Churchill

"Life doesn't get easier or more forgiving;
we get stronger and more resilient" —Dr. Steve Maraboli

NOTES

Be excellent

Perfection and excellence are two different things. Many argue that perfection does not exist. What you must do however, is aim to be excellent in everything you do.

Rather than strive to get everything right all the time, strive to excel in your own way. Give 100% effort every time!

ACTIVITY

In what areas would you improve if you were to develop a habit of being excellent?

....

....

How do you think being excellent would benefit you as a young adult in creating the life you desire?

....

....

QUOTE:

"We are what we repeatedly do. Excellence, then, is not an act, but a habit." —Aristotle

NOTES

Have Fun

I'm sure you'll agree that you enjoy a teacher who brings some element of fun to the class room. Having fun brings balance to life and levels out the stress of hard work and exams. When there's a healthy dose of fun incorporated in your day to day life, you will find that it's easier to accomplish difficult tasks.

Strive to have fun with everything you do. Fun and laughter is good medicine for the soul.

ACTIVITY

When and where do I have the most fun?

....

....

Am I always responsible when having fun, or do I lose myself and put myself in danger?

....

....

How can I incorporate fun in areas where it's more serious, like studying or group assignments?

....

....

QUOTE:

"There is no fear when you're having fun" —Will Thomas

NOTES

Affirmations

1. I will enjoy every second and every moment on this wonderful day.
2. I'm grateful for each new day. I wake up with purpose every day.
3. Today I wake up with joy in my soul and strength in my heart.
4. I am fearfully and wonderfully made.
5. God has plans for me, and they are all good plans.
6. I can do all things through Christ who strengthens me.
7. I have a plan, I have goals, and I'm working towards achieving them all.
8. I am smart and creative.
9. I'm bold. I accomplish anything I set out to, without giving in to external pressures.
10. I'm courageous. I never let fears or insecurities come between me and what I need to do.
11. I'm confident in every aspect.
12. I am gorgeous and attractive.
13. I am strong.
14. I am important and of high value.
15. I am focused and determined.
16. Nothing will stop me from achieving my goals.
17. I have good friends who support me, and I support them.
18. My family is one big joyous bunch, and we love and cherish each other.
19. I'm an important part of my family.
20. No weapon formed against me shall prosper.
21. I love every inch of my precious body.
22. I love life, and life loves me.
23. I am worthy of the best life has to offer.
24. I am blessed and highly favored.
25. Every day I am learning and becoming better and better.
26. My future is sparkling and bright.
27. I excel in school and life.
28. I love every bit of self-development.
29. Every day I am learning new skills that will help me become a responsible adult.
30. I am healthy and wise.
31. All my needs are met, and I'm learning how to best manage my money.
32. I don't need to be perfect, only excellent.
33. I forgive myself for my mistakes.
34. I am beautiful.

35. I deserve to be treated with love and kindness.
36. I believe in my abilities.
37. My words have power.
38. My opinion matters.
39. I dare to express my feelings.
40. I find solutions to my problems.
41. I am an over comer.
42. I can say no, and no will mean no.
43. This is only the beginning.
44. I'm excited about my future and everything that lies ahead.
45. My life is valuable.
46. Social media is not my source of strength.
47. I don't need to be liked.
48. I'm a good person.
49. I'm not lost, just creating and reinventing myself.
50. When I meet a bump in the road, I slow down, get over it and keep going.
51. It is not my job to please my friends.
52. I will travel and see the world.
53. I embrace change as a part of life.
54. I am safe and all is well.
55. Everything is working out for me.
56. I love learning.
57. My mind is alert.

NOTES

NOTES

NOTES

NOTES

NOTES

NOTES

NOTES

NOTES

NOTES

NOTES

NOTES

NOTES

NOTES

NOTES

NOTES

NOTES

NOTES

NOTES

NOTES

NOTES

NOTES

NOTES

NOTES

About the Author

Daneile Hicks-Burnett

Daneile is the co-founder of **Girl Stand Up!**, a non-profit project committed to improving the lives of girls through self-esteem and confidence building life tools. She has a passion for working with teen girls so they become the best version of themselves. Girl Stand Up hosts annual teen empowerment conferences, free of cost, to girls in Guyana, South America.